THE FABULOUS LOST & FOUND

AND THE LITTLE CZECH MOUSE

WRITTEN BY MARK PALLIS
ILLUSTRATED BY PETER BAYNTON

NEU WESTEND
— PRESS —

For Zdena, Nicole and Izzy - MP

For Hannah and Skye - PB

THE FABULOUS LOST & FOUND AND THE LITTLE CZECH MOUSE
Copyright text and images © 2023 Mark Pallis

First Printing, 2020
ISBN: 978-1-9160801-7-1
NeuWestendPress.com

THE FABULOUS LOST & FOUND

AND THE LITTLE CZECH MOUSE

WRITTEN BY MARK PALLIS
ILLUSTRATED BY PETER BAYNTON

NEU WESTEND
— PRESS —

In the middle of the big city is a tiny
yellow building. If anyone loses anything, this is
where it ends up.

It is called the Lost and Found.

Mr and Mrs Frog keep everything
safe, hoping that someday every lost
watch and bag and phone and toy
and shoe and cheesegrater will find
its owner again.

But the shop is very small. And
there are so many lost things. It
is all quite a squeeze, but still, it's
fabulous.

One sunny day, a little mouse walked in.

"Welcome," said Mrs Frog. "What have you lost?"

"Ztratila jsem čepici," said the mouse.

Mr and Mrs Frog could not speak Czech. They had no idea what the little mouse was saying.

What shall we do? they wondered.

Maybe she's lost an umbrella. Everyone loses an umbrella at least twice, thought Mr Frog.

"Have you lost this?" asked Mr Frog.

"Deštník? Ne," replied the mouse.

Then Mrs Frog remembered something
that had been handed in a few months ago...

"Is this yours?" Mrs Frog asked, holding up a chunk of cheese.

"Sýr? Ne. Smrdí!" said the mouse.

"Time to put that cheese in the bin dear," said Mr Frog.

"Maybe the word 'čepici' means coat," said Mr Frog.

"Now where did I put that nice yellow one?"

"Got it!" said Mr Frog.

"Kabát? Ne. Ztratila jsem čepici," said the mouse.

She was starting to feel a bit frustrated.

"We need to keep trying," said Mrs Frog.

Není to šála.

Nejsou to kalhoty.

Není to svetr.

Nejsou to sluneční brýle.

Nejsou to boty.

"Ztratila jsem čepici,"
said the mouse.

Nejsou to dvě kola.

Není to počítač.

Nejsou to tři knihy.

Nejsou to čtyři banány.

Není to pět klíčů.

It was no good. A fat wet tear rolled down the mouse's cheek.

"How about a nice cup of tea?" asked Mrs Frog kindly.

"Miluju čaj. Díky," replied the mouse. They sat together, sipping their tea and all feeling a bit sad.

Suddenly, the mouse realised she could try pointing.

She pointed at her head.

"Čepici!" she said.

"I've got it!" exclaimed Mrs Frog, leaping up.

"A wig of course!" said Mrs Frog.

"Není to paruka," said the mouse.

Není červená.

Není blond.

Není hnědá.

Není zelená.

Není vícebarevná.

"What about this?"
asked Mr Frog, pulling back
a curtain.

"Čepici!" exclaimed the
mouse.

"Ah, so 'čepici' means hat.
Wonderful!" Mr and Mrs
Frog cheered.

Moc vysoká.

Moc malá.

Moc velká.

Moc těsná.

"One hat left," said
Mrs Frog, reaching all
the way to the back of the
cupboard.

"It couldn't be this
old thing, could it?"

"Moje čepice!

Našla jsem čepici!

Děkuji mnohokrát," said the mouse.

And just like that, the mouse found her hat.

"Na shledanou," she said, as she skipped away.
"Na shledanou," replied Mr and Mrs Frog.

"I wonder who will come tomorrow?" said Mr Frog.
Mrs Frog put her arm around him.

"I don't know," she replied, giving him a squeeze,
"but whoever it is, we'll do our best to help."

LEARNING TO LOVE LANGUAGES

An additional language opens a child's mind, broadens their horizons and enriches their emotional life. Research has shown that the time between a child's birth and their sixth or seventh birthday is a "golden period" when they are most receptive to new languages. This is because they have an in-built ability to distinguish the sounds they hear and make sense of them. The Story-powered Language Learning Method taps into these natural abilities.

HOW THE STORY-POWERED LANGUAGE LEARNING METHOD WORKS

We create an emotionally engaging and funny story for children and adults to enjoy together, just like any other picture book. Studies show that social interaction, like enjoying a book together, is critical in language learning.

Through the story, we introduce a relatable character who speaks only in the new language. This helps build empathy and a positive attitude towards people who speak different languages. These are both important aspects in laying the foundations for lasting language acquisition in a child's life.

As the story progresses, the child naturally works with the characters to discover the meaning of a wide range of fun new words. Strategic use of humour ensures that this subconscious learning is rewarded with laughter; the child feels good and the first seeds of a lifelong love of languages are sown.

For more information and free downloads visit www.neuwestendpress.com

ALL THE BEAUTIFUL CZECH WORDS AND PHRASES FROM OUR STORY

ztratila jsem čepici	I've lost my hat	*hnědá*	brown
deštník	umbrella	*zelená*	green
sýr	cheese	*vícebarevná*	multicoloured
smrdí	it stinks	*ne*	no
kabát	coat	*moc vysoká*	too tall
šála	scarf	*moc velká*	too big
kalhoty	trousers	*moc malá*	too small
sluneční brýle	sunglasses	*moc těsná*	too tight
svetr	sweater	*našla jsem čepici*	I've found my hat
boty	shoes	*na shledanou*	goodbye
jeden	one		
dvě	two		
tři	three		
čtyři	four		
pět	five		
počítač	computer		
knihy	books		
klíčů	keys		
banány	bananas		
kola	bicycles		
Miluju čaj	I love tea		
díky	thanks		
děkuji	thank you		
paruka	wig		
červená	red		
blond	blond		

You can learn more words and phrases with these hilarious, heartwarming stories from NEU WESTEND — PRESS —

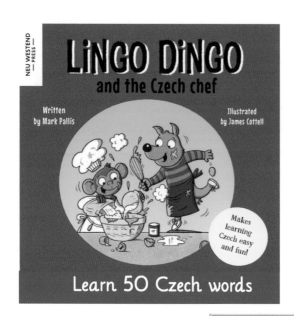

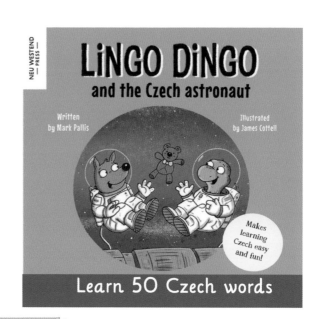

To download your FREE certifcate, and more cool stuff, visit www.markpallis.com

These books are also available in over 50 different languages! What language will you learn next?

"I want people to be so busy laughing, they don't realise they're learning!"

Crab and Whale is the bestselling story of how a little Crab helps a big Whale. It's carefully designed to help even the most energetic children find a moment of calm and focus. It also includes a special mindful breathing exercise and affirmation for children.

Featured as one of Mindful.org's 'Seven Mindful Children's books'

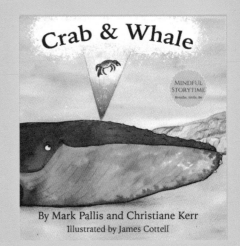

Do you call them hugs or cuddles?

In this funny, heartwarming story, you will laugh out loud as two loveable gibbons try to figure out if a hug is better than a cuddle and, in the process, learn how to get along.

A perfect story for anyone who loves a hug (or a cuddle!)

www.markpallis.com

Printed in Great Britain
by Amazon

46196300R00023